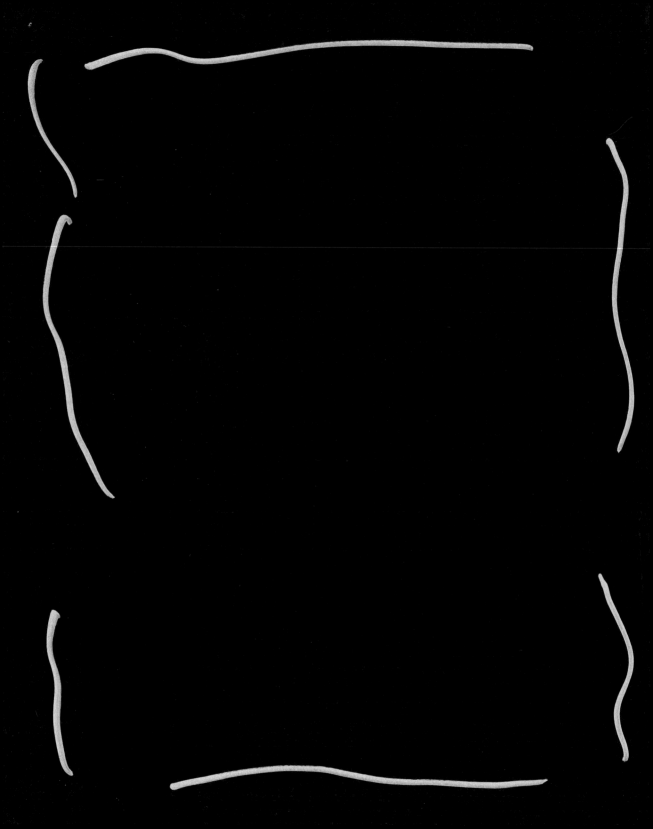

Lands of Mystery

by Judith Herbst

Lerner Publications Company • Minneapolis

Lerner Publications Company
A division of Lerner Publishing Group
241 First Avenue North
Minneapolis, Minnesota 55401 U.S.A.

Website address: www.lernerbooks.com

Library of Congress Cataloging-in-Publication Data

Herbst, Judith.
    Lands of mystery / by Judith Herbst.
        p.   cm. — (The unexplained)
    Includes index.
    ISBN: 0–8225–1630–6 (lib. bdg. : alk. paper)
    1. Atlantis. 2. Pyramids of Giza (Egypt). 3. Roanoke Colony I. Title. II. Series:
    Unexplained (Lerner Publications Company)
    GN751.H35 2005
    001.94—dc22   2004004515

Manufactured in the United States of America
1 2 3 4 5 6 – JR – 10 09 08 07 06 05

Table of Contents

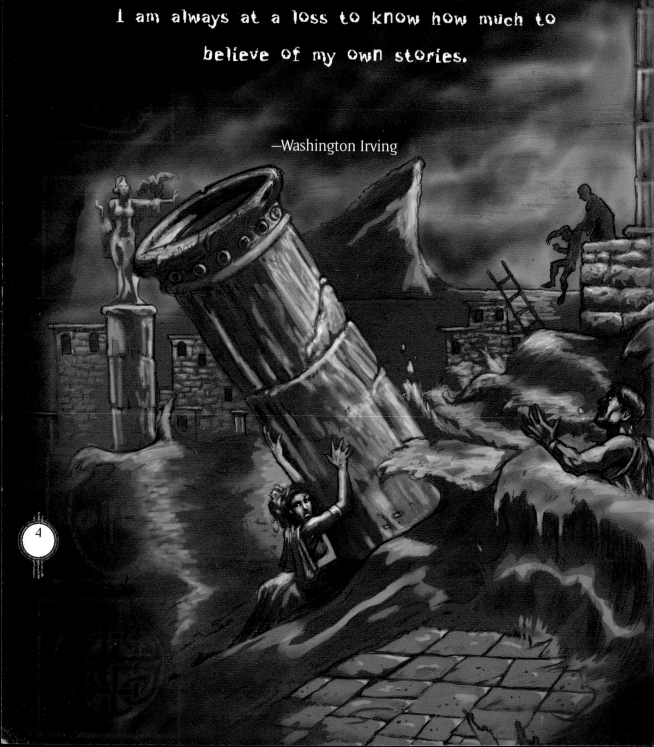

I am always at a loss to know how much to
believe of my own stories.

—Washington Irving

4

CHAPTER 1

ATLANTIS

"And on your left," said our tour guide in an accent I couldn't quite place, "you will see the rock formations known as the Pillars of Hercules."

I craned my neck to get a better view, but it didn't help. I couldn't see a thing. "Where?" I shouted.

The tour guide ignored me. He was following a very tight script. "And just beyond the Pillars," he continued, "far, far below the waves, at the very bottom of the Atlantic Ocean, lies the sunken continent of Atlantis."

My fellow travelers oohed and aahed and gurgled just a bit, but I'm no fool. I knew what this guy was doing.

"Hey!" I screamed. I don't normally yell like this, but the situation seemed to be calling for it. "Atlantis is a myth. Plato made it up. No such island. Never existed. Fake-a-roo."

Every head turned to glare at me. I was ruining their vacation. The tour guide narrowed his eyes. "Then suppose you tell us all," he rudely snarled, "why so many people have spent so much time searching for it."

I shrugged. "Beats me," I said.

The tour guide fumed for a while and then leveled his finger at me. "Explain your charges against Atlantis!" he boomed. And this is what I said.

>> Plato Gets the Ball Rolling

The whole thing started around 400 B.C., with the ancient Greek philosopher Plato. Plato earned fame, but not necessarily fortune, writing a series of dialogues. The dialogues weren't plays, exactly, but more like discussions. Plato's characters were students who sat around talking about stuff like justice and truth. Socrates, their teacher, always started the sessions with a question, and the students tossed ideas back and forth. They never really settled anything, but they seemed to have a pretty good time anyway.

Well, one day Socrates brought up the subject of the ideal society. He described what he thought it would be like but then decided it probably wouldn't work in the real world. So he asked his students for suggestions.

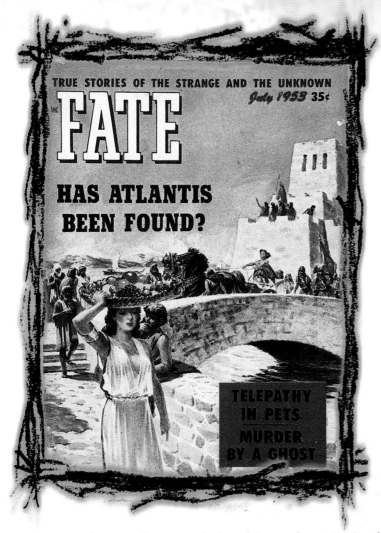

The July 1953 issue of *Fate* magazine featured this illustration of Atlantis on its cover. The mystery of Atlantis has intrigued humans for centuries.

It just so happened that his student Critias had heard about a utopian society that supposedly existed about 9,000 years earlier. The place was called Atlantis, he said, and it was located beyond the Pillars of Hercules in the Atlantic Ocean. Atlantis, said Critias, was bigger than Syria and Asia combined. Plato's Asia was actually Asia Minor, which we call Turkey. But it was still pretty darned big, if you ask me.

EUROPE

ATLANTIC
OCEAN

GREECE

THERA

ASIA
MINOR
(TURKEY)

Mediterranean Sea

Pillars of Hercules

CRETE

SYRIA

AFRICA

"Well, we didn't ask you," said the tour guide.

I made a face and continued.

Atlantis had it all. There were gardens and palaces, towers and gates, and jeweled buildings that gleamed like fire. There were mountains, meadows, and fields with soil that was deliciously fertile. The people lived in luxury and were governed by just rulers. The place was perfect, and the Atlanteans knew it. But instead of simply appreciating what they had, they let it go to their heads. They allowed their wealth to corrupt their hearts. They lusted after power and began to ignore the laws that had shaped their fine society. In other words, they made a mess of things.

The gods, of course, saw all this and didn't like it one bit. Zeus, the king of the gods, was flat-out disgusted, so he decided to punish the

The ancient Greeks believed that all natural disasters, such as storms, earthquakes, and volcanoes, were created by angry gods to punish humans. Did Zeus, the king of the Greek gods, conjure an earthquake that sank Atlantis?

Atlanteans in no uncertain terms. "I will have order!" he thundered, and he shook Atlantis with the biggest, meanest earthquake he could muster up. But he didn't get order. What he got instead was complete destruction, because Atlantis promptly sank into the sea and was never heard from again.

The tour guide folded his arms. "So what makes you think this story is fiction?"

This guy was too much.

"All right," he said. "Maybe Plato exaggerated a little, but the legend could very easily have been based on truth. Many legends are."

I considered this. "Present your evidence!" I demanded, and this is what he said.

>> Who'd Like to Vote for the Minoans?

If we're going to find Atlantis, we have to begin at the end. Plato says that Atlantis was destroyed by earthquakes and floods, and then the whole kit and caboodle disappeared into the sea. I grant you, this sounds impossible, but in the 19th century, the island of Krakatau did exactly that. Well, maybe not *exactly* that, but pretty close.

Krakatau was a volcanic island in the Sundra Strait between Sumatra and Java in Indonesia. In May 1883, the island was rocked by several powerful earthquakes. Three months later, in the middle of the night, the volcano erupted with such force that the blast literally ripped the mountain apart. It hurled a gigantic black cloud of material high into

the air, where it rolled and churned, sparking like an exploded electrical transformer. As the mountain crashed into the sea, it raised monster waves 50 feet high. The waves pulsed outward, flooding coastlines 8,000 miles away and drowning thousands of people. When the dust cleared, the ash

In 1883 a gigantic volcano erupted on the island of Krakatau, ripping the island in two. Could Atlantis have suffered the same fate thousands of years ago?

settled, and the sea stopped boiling, all that was left of Krakatau was a six-square-mile speck of land—less than half the island's original size.

"So you're saying that Krakatau was Atlantis?" I said.

The tour guide snorted. "Not at all. I was merely giving an example. May I continue?"

I nodded and he did.

"It just so happens that a civilization *did* vanish not too far from here."

"In the Atlantic Ocean?" I wanted to know.

"Er . . . no," he said. "In the Mediterranean, but that's still beyond the Pillars of Hercules."

"No, no, no," I said. "You're cheating. For Plato, who lived in Greece, 'beyond' meant west of the Pillars, not east. If he'd meant east, he would have said something like 'right here, practically next door, just a teensy bit south of us.'"

I could tell the tour guide was miffed. "May I finish, please?" he snarled.

"Sure," I said, but we both knew he was in trouble already.

We must go back (the tour guide continued) about 6,000 years, to when the first people came to the mountainous island of Crete. The climate was gentle and the land was rich, and before long, permanent villages began to spring up. By 3000 B.C., Knossos—the most famous of them—had become a town and then a fabulous city. The first of many grand palaces was built some-time around 2000 B.C.

The Minoans, as the people came to be called, were industrious and cre-ative, elegant and refined. They loved the arts. They wrote books and stud-ied and developed a culture that was far and away more advanced than those of other Mediterranean peoples. They raised sheep and crafted tex-tiles and jewelry. Their sculpture and pottery were breathtaking. Their simple homes were transformed into art museums with brilliant paint-ings that adorned the limestone walls. Who knows to what heights the Minoans could have climbed had it not been for a single catastrophe?

It occurred, not on Crete, but 80 miles away on the island of Thera. Perhaps Thera's volcano gave fair warning of what was to come. For months it may

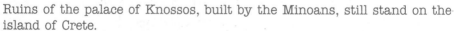
Ruins of the palace of Knossos, built by the Minoans, still stand on the island of Crete.

BULLY FOR CRETE

The Minoans did not call themselves Minoans. The name comes from Crete's King Minos, although nobody knows if he was real or fictional.

According to legend, the sea god Poseidon had sent Minos a white bull. Minos agreed to sacrifice it as an act of respect. But he pulled a fast one and substituted another bull at the last minute. Poseidon, being a god, naturally saw this and took revenge. He "put lust in the heart" of Minos's wife Pasiphae for the bull who had escaped death. The resulting offspring was a minotaur, a monster with the body of a human and the head of a bull. (*Taurus* is Greek for "bull.")

The minotaur wound up spending his days in a labyrinth, a maze of winding passages. He ate maidens and young men who were tossed over the walls every nine years. When it was Theseus's turn to be sacrificed, the kid had no intention of lying down on the minotaur's dinner plate. He promptly slew the monster. It's a racy story with plenty of blood and guts. That's Greek mythology for you.

have huffed and puffed and belched thick, black smoke signals. But the people would have ignored it. If they had never seen an eruption, they would not have known the kind of disaster that lay in wait.

The day dawned, 3,500 years ago. If the winds were right, the Minoans awoke to the smell of sulfur from across the sea. But it was the Therans who heard the roar. It rolled upward from the center of the earth. After a few horrifying hours that must have seemed like forever, the volcano burst apart in a

In 1967 archaeologists on Thera uncovered ancient Minoan ruins buried by volcanic rock and ash. Some people consider the findings to be proof that Atlantis did exist.

titanic explosion, gouging out a massive chunk of the island. Hot ash rained down in a fiery torrent, and the shock wave raised a mighty wall of water that moved with deadly intent toward Crete. Poisonous gases followed.

The sea around Crete would have receded before the wave's arrival, sucking in its breath and laying the sandy bottom bare. But even those who might have understood had nowhere to run. The massive wave crashed down upon the land, drowning the people, the palaces, the cities and fields, ending forever the Minoan civilization.

Was Crete Atlantis? The similarities are too great to ignore.

"Oh yeah?" I said. "What about the differences? The destruction of Crete was much too recent. Critias said he heard the story from his grandfather, who got it from a poet named Solon, who heard it from an Egyptian priest, who said it was 9,000 years old."

"Exaggeration," snapped the tour guide. "Writers do it all the time."

I smirked. "But you have also placed Atlantis in the wrong spot."

"So what? People have searched all over the globe for Atlantis—in Nigeria, Bolivia, Morocco, the Yucatán Peninsula in Mexico, Brazil, the Sahara Desert, and even Antarctica!"

"You forgot Bimini Island," I said.

The tour guide's eyes lit up. "Oooo," he said, "that's right!" And he was off and running.

>> Atlantis of the Bahamas

Edgar Cayce is probably one of the most popular psychics who ever lived. This doesn't mean, of course, that he could actually see into the future—only that a lot of people *thought* he could. At any rate, Cayce claimed to have gotten the scoop on Atlantis while he was in some of his famous trances. The island, he said, did not sink near the Pillars of Hercules. It went down in either the Sargasso Sea or the Bahamas.

In the North Atlantic Ocean off the east coast of Bermuda *(below)* lies the Sargasso Sea, named after the Portuguese word for the seaweed found there.

Well, nobody really liked the idea that Atlantis might be in the Sargasso Sea. The Sargasso, which covers much of the central North Atlantic Ocean, is a very nasty place. In addition to being the spawning ground for eels, it has vast beds of floating seaweed—a scuba diver's worst nightmare. It is all too easy to become helplessly entangled in the stuff. So it was to the Bahamas that underwater explorer David Zink chose to go in 1975 to look for the lost continent of Atlantis. And what he found almost knocked his flippers off. There, on the seafloor off the coast of Bimini Island, lay what looked like stone roadways and the remains of buildings. Had Atlantis, at long last, been found?

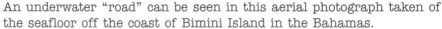

An underwater "road" can be seen in this aerial photograph taken of the seafloor off the coast of Bimini Island in the Bahamas.

"No," I said. "It had not. According to geologists—which David Zink is not—the so-called Bimini road is a natural formation. What appears to be paving stones set at right angles to each other is actually beach rock, formed when seawater containing the mineral calcium carbonate washes over sand grains and cements them together. The result is a hard, rocky block that breaks easily in straight lines. It's actually quite common."

"Oh," said the tour guide. He looked defeated, probably because he had been.

"Hey, listen," I said in an effort to cheer him up. "I'll bet you didn't know this. Edgar Cayce also said that some Atlanteans managed to escape the disaster, and that the priests buried their sacred documents under the paws of the Sphinx in Egypt."

"So what's your point?" said the tour guide.

I smiled in a smooth Cheshire cat way. "Some people think that the Sphinx is much older than the pyramids. They believe it was built by an advanced civilization that existed 5,000 years before the Egyptians. They also think that there is a hollow chamber under the paws. And if that is so," I whispered, "and ancient scrolls are found there, then perhaps everything Plato wrote was true. Atlantis did exist."

"Oh, my," breathed the tour guide, as a dreamy look swept over his face. "Then clearly, Egypt must be our next stop."

CHAPTER 2
SECRETS
OF THE PHARAOHS

"Did aliens build the Egyptian pyramids?" our tour guide asked.

I rolled my eyes.

"No!" he cried triumphantly. "They did not!"

Well, that was certainly a relief. I had really started to wonder about this guy.

"Behold one of humankind's greatest achievements!" he said with a dramatic sweep of his arm. "The pyramids at Giza!"

We beheld the pyramids in respectful silence.

"The largest is the Pyramid of Khufu," he continued, "also called the Great Pyramid, built around 2540 B.C. Its original height was 481 feet, but it is now 30 feet shorter because the capstone that once sat on top is missing. Its base covers 13 acres, and the four sides are almost precisely oriented to the four cardinal points of the compass. More than two million stone blocks were used in its construction, and . . . "

"Get on with it!" I shouted. "Nobody cares about all those boring statistics. Get to the mysteries! Get to the spooky stuff! Get to the mummies!"

The tour guide glared at me. I seemed to be his worst nightmare. He expelled air. "All right," he said at last. "Mummies it is."

"Hoora-a-ay!" shouted the group.

"But first . . ."

Everyone groaned.

". . . I'd like to say a few words about Khufu."

Khufu (near left) ruled Egypt from 2589 to 2566 B.C. He built the largest of the three pyramids at Giza, Egypt (facing page).

The Bent Pyramid at Dashur, built by the Egyptian king Snefru, got its name because of its crooked sides.

>> A Pyramid for the Ages

Khufu's father, Snefru, was the first king of Egypt's Fourth Dynasty. Snefru, by all accounts, was a pretty decent ruler with a particular fondness for pyramids. And since he also had tons of money, lots of slaves, and absolute power, he built two of them. They're a few miles south at Dashur, so you can't see them from here. But take my word for it, they're very impressive. Nobody was ever going to forget Snefru, that was for sure!

Well, when Khufu succeeded his father and became king, he was not about to let the old man have the biggest pyramids in Egypt. So he ordered the construction of a massive pyramid at the edge of the desert on the Giza plateau. This, he told himself, was going to be AWESOME, a pyramid for the ages.

That it most certainly was.

The Great Pyramid at Giza has stood in the sun-blasted desert along the banks of the Nile River for more than 4,500 years. Its 30-foot capstone, thought to have been granite, is long gone. The white limestone facing has been looted for local building projects. Thieves, believing the pyramid contained a hidden treasure, tried to hack their way in below the original entrance on the north face. But Khufu's monument remains without equal, the greatest of all pyramids ever built. Snefru would have either been very proud of his kid or insanely jealous.

The tour guide paused, and I reminded him about the mummies, but he waved me off. "Not yet," he said. He resumed his narrative.

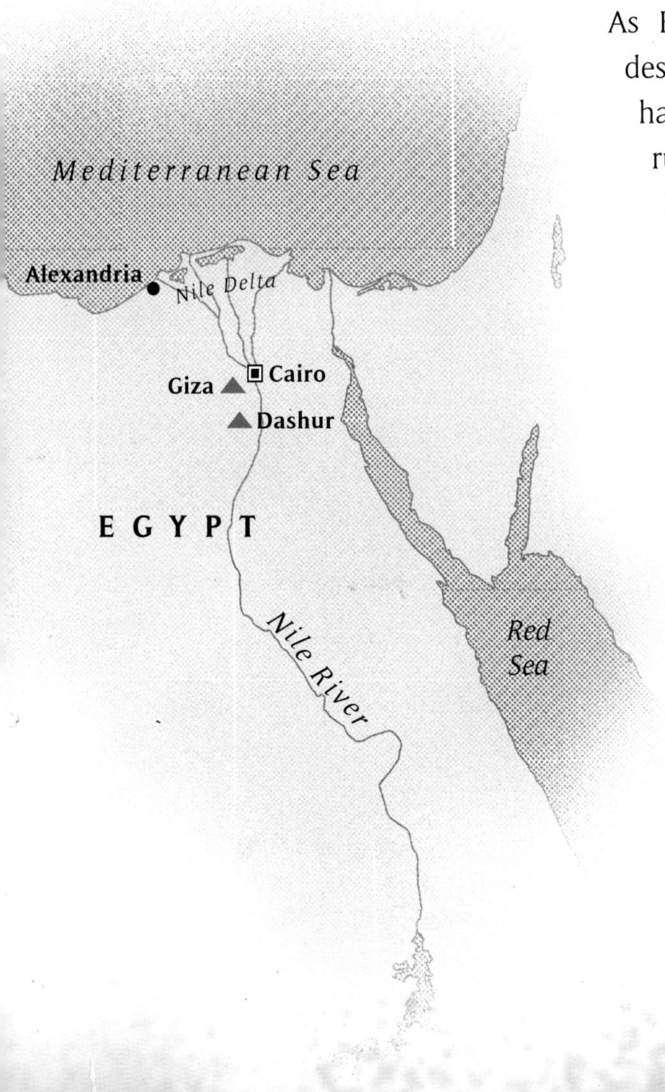

As Khufu's tomb rose from the desert floor, block by two-and-a-half-ton block, the king must have rubbed his hands in silent glee. Deep into this massive structure, his mummified body would be carried in a grand procession. A burial chamber filled with magnificent furniture and jeweled objects would be waiting for him. Rich foods would be laid out upon a delicately carved table.

Mediterranean Sea

Alexandria
Nile Delta

Giza ▲ ■ Cairo
▲ Dashur

E G Y P T

Nile River

Red Sea

Maybe
It Was the Purr

It is no secret that the ancient Egyptians loved cats. Just look at the Sphinx, whose body is that of a reclining lion, mighty and proud, with massive paws outstretched. Bast and Pasht were two forms of a cat-headed Egyptian goddess who represented life and fruitfulness. Like a cat, she could be warlike or mellow and cool, depending on her mood and the situation.

What was it about the cat that the Egyptians so admired, or perhaps even envied? It might have been the cat's lithe body and its remarkable sense of balance. It might have been its ability to kill quickly and efficiently. It might have been its silky coat, its astonishing eyes, or the fact that you never really know what a cat is thinking. Or it might have been the purr.

Thousands of cat mummies have been discovered in Egypt, a clear indication that the deceased had no intention of leaving this world without taking along the family cat. Mouse mummies have also been found in a number of tombs—a box lunch for a beloved companion.

His favorite palace cat would be there, mummified and hon-ored, enclosed in a small coffin. There would be flowers and spices, and nearby, the beautiful boat that would carry him to the next world.

Khufu could hear the construction noise and smell the sweat of the workers, but he cared little for their suffering. It was not his concern how they cut and transported the enormous blocks of stone from the distant quarries. He may have watched them lift each mono-lith to dizzying heights, assured by Hemon, his architect, that the alignment would be perfect. But it hardly mattered to him that slaves were sometimes crushed when a block slipped or a rope broke. His pyramid would be finished exactly the way he wanted it.

It took 20 years. Nobody knows how it was done. But when Khufu died, the pyramid was ready for him.

They brought him to the embalmers, who removed most of his internal organs and packed the empty cavity with sawdust and cloth. They washed his body with water from the Nile, dried it out with a mineral called natron, and sprinkled it with sweet-smelling spices. They coated strips of linen with sticky resin and began to wrap the body, tucking rings and other small objects between the layers. The procedure took 70

Many mummies have been lost or destroyed, including Khufu's, but some remain. This is the mummy of Ramses II, one of the greatest kings of ancient Egypt.

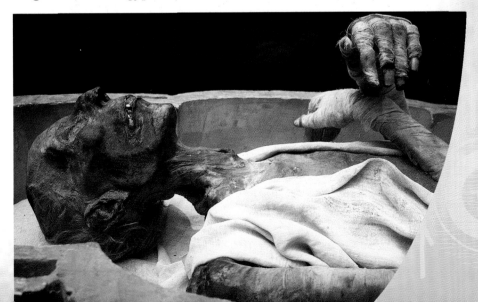

Egyptians in a funeral procession carry furniture and other goods into a tomb.

days. When all was complete, priests read text from the Book of the Dead, a guide intended to help the deceased reach a happy afterlife.

"Here come plants sprung from the earth, flax, and restoratives. They come to you in the form of a precious shroud. They preserve you in the form of bandages. They make you grow larger in the form of linen."

Khufu was carried across the sand in a brightly painted coffin. His dazzling white pyramid blazed like a heavenly fire pointing to the stars.

"Your legs will carry you to the Eternal Abode and your hands will carry you as far as the place of infinite duration."

The procession entered at the north face of the pyramid. The narrow passage descended several feet and then began to climb. Khufu's burial chamber lay almost at the very heart of the pyramid. The second king of the Fourth Dynasty was placed in a stone sarcophagus, cut long ago from a single block of granite. Then the burial party made its way out.

"Hold it right there!" I shouted.

The tour guide blinked like a confused owl.

"I must say, I'm not impressed. A spoiled rich king, a gigantic pyramid, and one measly mummy—without any gruesome pictures, I might add."

"I couldn't show you pictures," said the tour guide. "Khufu's mummy wasn't in the tomb. Grave robbers got to it."

"Cancel the one measly mummy," I muttered.

"I am not, however, finished," said the tour guide. "I believe you also asked for mysteries."

"I did," said I, rather stiffly.

The tour guide's eyes twinkled. "Then take a look at this cross section of Khufu's pyramid."

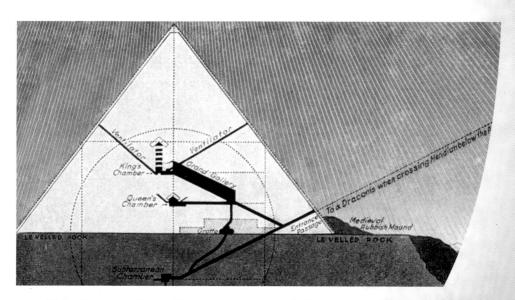

This diagram shows the arrangement of chambers, passages, and air shafts (ventilators) inside the Great Pyramid.

"Right here," he said, tapping the page, "and here," another tap, "are two narrow shafts that lead from Khufu's burial chamber straight through the pyramid to the outside. The shafts rise at fairly steep angles—31 degrees for the northern shaft and 45 degrees for the southern shaft. They start about three feet above the floor of the chamber. Curious, don't you think?"

We all agreed that it was.

"Some have suggested that the openings might be air shafts. But a mummy doesn't need fresh air, so the shafts must have been cut for another reason."

"Can we guess?" I wanted to know.

"No."

Several feet below Khufu's burial chamber (he continued), there is another, smaller chamber. Scholars think Khufu had planned to be buried there but changed his mind. So the chamber was never completed. But guess what. This chamber has two unfinished shafts, also cut into the north and south walls. The plot thickens, does it not?

We all agreed that it did.

In an attempt to solve this mystery of the shafts, we must leap forward into the next generation. The first king to succeed Khufu was his son Djedefre, who didn't live very long. For whatever reason, Djedefre built his pyramid five miles north of Giza. But Khafre, son number two, was a kid with vision. Khafre elected to stick with the Giza plan and set his pyramid next to his dad's. He's also credited with building the Sphinx, but more about that later. The third and smallest pyramid in the complex belonged to Menkaure, one of Khafre's sons. So we have three pyramids, one after another, but not in a perfectly straight line. The third one is off a little. Does that matter? Oh, you bet it does. This, ladies and gentlemen, is the Giza complex as seen from the air.

Does it remind you of anything? No? Okay. Here's a hint. One of the very oldest and most important of the Egyptian gods was Horus, whose

As seen from the air, the three pyramids at Giza do not line up perfectly. Considering the Egyptians' perfectionism, this could not have been a mistake.

The stars in Orion's belt are not perfectly straight either. Did they inspire the placement of the pyramids at Giza?

name means "he who is above." Horus was the sky god, but he was also associated with the constellation Orion. Look at Orion's belt. Three stars, not quite in a straight line. The third one is off a little. . . .

"Yikes!" I cried. "Are you suggesting that the pyramids at Giza were built to match the stars in the belt of Orion?"

The tour guide actually giggled.

The ancient Egyptians (he continued) believed that their kings were direct descendants of the god Rā, who rode across the sky each day as the rising and setting sun. This was what you might call having connections in high places. It meant that when a king died, he would return to the sky and take his place among the stars. So we now come to the mysterious shafts in the Great Pyramid.

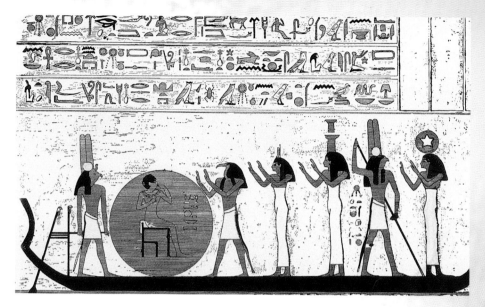

An illustration depicts the sun god, Rā, embarking on his journey across the sky.

"I want to guess!" I shouted loud enough for Khufu himself to hear me. "The shafts were the way the king's soul got out of the pyramid and into the sky!"

"Better than that," said the tour guide. "At the time of the Fourth Dynasty, the southern shaft in Khufu's burial chamber pointed directly to the first star in Orion's belt. What an astounding feat of engineering! A building this size, made of enormous stone slabs, each weighing tons! How were they able to align it with such precision?" The tour guide shook his head in wonderment, deeply impressed.

"And the northern shaft," he continued after a respectful moment of silence, "pointed directly to the first star in the constellation Draco, the dragon. But the Egyptians didn't see a dragon; they saw a hippopotamus. And in Egyptian hieroglyphic writing, the hippopotamus symbolized the heavens."

"And the unfinished chamber?" I said.

"The northern shaft would have pointed to Sirius, the brightest star in the sky, and the southern, to Ursa Minor—the Little Dipper—home of the North Star."

"What about the Sphinx?" I wanted to know.

"Well," said the tour guide, slowly rubbing his chin. "The Sphinx is another story entirely."

>> The Riddle of the Sphinx

The Sphinx was supposedly built by Khafre, Khufu's son, which would make it about 4,500 years old. But a handful of scientists, writers, and others are not so sure that the Sphinx was Khafre's idea. The head is certainly Khafre's, but the body is that of a lion. Why would Khafre have had himself portrayed as a lion? Well, in the mythology of many cultures, the lion is the symbol of royal power. One that is 240 feet long, 66 feet high, and carved from a single block of stone certainly gets the point across. But for the Egyptians, a lion was also the guardian of the gates of the underworld.

So let's suppose the Sphinx was not originally a sphinx at all, but a lion. And let's suppose it was already there when Khafre became king. Khafre then decides to build his pyramid beside his father's. He adds a temple and a road that leads from it directly to the lion. The lion, guardian of the gates of the underworld, now stands at the gates of his pyramid complex. Finally, Khafre doubles the fun and has his artisans turn the lion's head into his own head.

A side view of the Sphinx shows its lion body topped with the head of Khafre. Was the head carved centuries after the original sculpture was created?

"Well, that's a cute story," I said, "but it needs some support."

"Then support I shall provide. You may have noticed that the Sphinx is somewhat weather-beaten."

"Well, sitting out in the desert and getting blasted by sand for 4,500 years will do that," I said.

The tour guide chuckled. "Perhaps it was not sand that eroded the sides of the Sphinx. Perhaps it was water."

"In the desert?" I snorted. "Don't be ridiculous."

In the 1990s, Boston University professor of geology Robert Schoch found breaks in the rock of which the Sphinx is constructed. He says the cracks were made by running water from heavy rains. At first this seems impossible, and it is if the Sphinx is 4,500 years old. For hundreds of centuries, most

Professor Robert Schoch

of Egypt has been a desert with an annual rainfall of about one inch. But if we go back farther than that, to about 6000 B.C., we find a very different climate. About 8,000 to 10,000 years ago, it actually rained here—and rained a lot.

Schoch believes that the front and sides of the Sphinx are between 7,000 and 9,000 years old. (He agrees with the Egyptologists that the carved human head is from Khafre's reign.) At that time, the Egyptians were using stone tools and hunting down their food with bows and arrows. They weren't capable of such a construction feat. This would suggest, of course, that someone other than the Egyptians built the Sphinx. And these people must have been fabulous, indeed. Who were these amazingly advanced people?

The tour guide paused and wiggled his eyebrows playfully.

I knew what was coming. "Don't say it!" I shouted, covering my ears with my hands. "Don't say the *A* word! I was only joking!"

"Some surveys were done," the tour guide continued, "on the bedrock beneath the paws of the Sphinx, and you won't believe what they found."

"The lost continent of Atlantis," I said sarcastically.

"No. Anomalies."

"What? What are those?"

"Irregularities. Strange formations that shouldn't be there."

I narrowed my eyes. "Like little chambers, perhaps?"

"Perhaps."

"Where the fleeing Atlanteans could have stashed their sacred scrolls?"

The tour guide shrugged. "Maybe."

"So what happens now?" I said. "We hang around and wait for someone to dig under the Sphinx?"

"Phooey!" said the tour guide. "Of course not. We have to be in North Carolina by morning." With those words, he led us across the sands to the waiting bus.

CHAPTER 3

THE LOST COLONY OF ROANOKE

"Ah," said the tour guide, rubbing his hands as if he were about to dig into a delicious meal. "The scene of the crime!"

I looked around but failed to see any criminal activity. There were fishing boats in Roanoke Sound and vacationers in Bermuda shorts. A kid was selling ice cream from a cart with a green umbrella. Everything looked quite hunky-dory to me. "Explain yourself," I said, and this is how he began.

In late June of 1585, a small group of adventurers from England arrived on an island off the coast of what would one day be North Carolina. Their plan was to establish the first settlement in America, a place that was, to say the least, pretty wild. These guys had grit, though, and immediately set about building a fort. By all accounts, it was a reasonably good fort, and the settlers seemed to be off to a rousing start. Wooden houses with brick chimneys and thatched roofs soon followed. Before long, Thomas Hariot was gathering information on native plants and animals for a book he was going to write. The newcomers were also getting along quite well with the Roanoke Island Indians, who had been gracious enough to teach everyone how to smoke tobacco.

There was, however, one small problem. Nobody knew the first thing about hunting, fishing, or planting. There were able carpenters in the group. There were brick makers, thatchers, and soldiers. But there were

At first, the Roanoke Island Indians were willing to share their knowledge of hunting, fishing, and farming with the colonists.

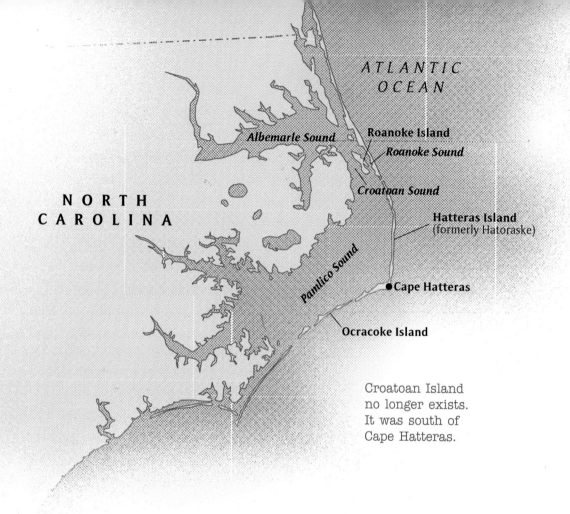

ATLANTIC
OCEAN

NORTH
CAROLINA

Albemarle Sound

Roanoke Island

Roanoke Sound

Croatoan Sound

Hatteras Island
(formerly Hatoraske)

Pamlico Sound

●Cape Hatteras

Ocracoke Island

Croatoan Island
no longer exists.
It was south of
Cape Hatteras.

also entirely too many proper English gentlemen who thought that food simply appeared on their plates as if by magic. All one had to do was sit down at the table, tuck a linen napkin into one's collar, and wait. And this is precisely how the colonists figured things would be on the American island of Roanoke. "English ships will arrive in a timely manner," they all said, "and bring us food and supplies!" This, to say the least, was not a well-thought-out plan.

During the first year, the Indians shared their harvest with the bumbling colonists. They taught them how to build traps and showed them the best places to catch fish. But the Englishmen were clearly out of their element. Like spoiled little kids, they began to whine for their soft beds and elegant sitting rooms. They eventually managed to annoy the Indians so much that their once good relationship broke down and nobody liked anybody anymore.

When the promised supply ships failed to appear, the colonists started to sweat. They found themselves going hungry between the spring planting and the summer and fall harvests. And somebody was raiding their fish traps. So Ralph Lane, who had been made governor of Roanoke Island, sent some of the settlers to the outer islands to watch for passing ships.

Meanwhile, Sir Richard Grenville, who had dragged everybody to Roanoke in the first place, was back in England working on the supply

ship problem. Unfortunately, he couldn't seem to get the ball rolling because England was in the process of going to war with Spain. But it just so happened that the daring explorer Sir Francis Drake had just arrived off Roanoke with a fleet of 23 ships. What luck! thought Lane, who headed out for Drake's ship and tried to get help for his starving colonists.

Sir Francis Drake

Well, Drake was a good guy, so he offered Lane a ship, a few small boats, and enough supplies to keep the colony going for another month. Or, if the settlers preferred, he would give everyone on the island free passage home.

This was a tough decision for Lane, who didn't want to abandon Roanoke. But when he realized there was really no place around the island to anchor the ship Drake had offered, he decided it was best to throw in the towel. So on June 18, 1586, Lane and all the Roanoke adventurers headed back to England.

Two weeks later, Grenville showed up with three supply ships and found the settlement abandoned. He had no idea what had happened to the colonists, but he certainly wasn't going to just turn around and go home. The British had fought hard to colonize America, and Grenville felt they ought to try to live there. So he left 15 men on the island as a way of saying "we've got dibs on this place" and went back to England.

"Stop!" I yelled. "Haven't you forgotten something?"

The tour guide blinked. "I beg your pardon?"

"The crime! Where's the crime?"

"Oh. That. Well, actually, nobody knows for sure if a crime was committed. Could have been, but then again, maybe not. Hard to tell."

I tapped my foot.

"It's quite a mystery, though."

"Then let's hear it!" I demanded, and this is what the tour guide said.

The second group of Roanoke colonists, which arrived in 1587, included women and children.

>> Gone!

Sir Walter Raleigh had been the recruiter for the first Roanoke Island settlement, and he also organized the second batch of colonists. This time, though, the group included farmers, women, and children.

"Good thinking," I said.

"But not good enough," said the tour guide in a very gloomy tone. He went on. "The ships arrived early July 1587."

"What about the 15 guys they left on the island? Were they okay?" I wanted to know.

"Not exactly. They were gone. They found the bones of one of the men, killed, they figured, by the Indians. But they never proved it. No one knows what happened to the rest. The fort had been destroyed, but the houses were still standing. Any ideas?"

We shook our heads.

It was not a good start, but the colonists decided to remain on Roanoke anyway and try to make a go of it. This time, though, the Indians were a lot less tolerant of the newcomers, and things got out of hand pretty fast. In fact, a war would very likely have broken out if it hadn't been for an Indian named Manteo, who stepped in and calmed everyone down. It was, however, an uneasy peace.

A month passed, and the colonists began to discuss the idea of moving their settlement to the mainland. But supplies were running low, and John White, whom Sir Walter Raleigh had made governor, knew he had to get back to England to reload, so to speak. (Obviously they

If At First You Don't Succeed . . .

When it came to colonizing America, the British were certainly not quitters. In May 1607, they reached Virginia and established the colony of Jamestown (in honor of King James I). By 1619 they had a government set up and were happily growing tobacco. But it hadn't been easy. Because the area they had chosen for their settlement was marshy, many died of mosquito-borne diseases. The settlement burned to the ground in 1608. In 1610 almost everybody was ready to call it quits. But that year Baron De La Warr brought encouragement and supplies, and the group pushed on.

In 1620 the *Mayflower* delivered a hardy bunch of settlers to the shores of Cape Cod in Massachusetts. About a month later, a boarding party arrived at Plymouth. Half the settlers died that first year, but those who remained were determined to succeed. In 1633 the town of Plymouth was officially recognized as the seat of Plymouth Colony. And the rest, as they say, is history.

Moral of the story: Never give up.

hadn't learned a thing from the first disaster.) So White worked out a signal with the colonists that would let him know if they had run into trouble or decided for any other reason to move the colony before he returned. They were to carve a Maltese cross or a sign of distress into the bark of a tree.

White set sail on August 27, 1587. When he reached England, he found the war with Spain in full swing. "Sorry, old boy," they told him. "We can't spare any ships."

"But you don't understand," White groaned, concerned for the welfare of his little colony. Yes, they said, they did, but national defense was far more important than some dinky little colony on the other side of the Atlantic. So White bit his lip nervously and waited. Finally, eight months after his arrival, the queen's Privy Council scrounged up a couple of small ships for the supply run to America. But unfortunately, White never quite made it. Instead, he preferred to chase after Spanish treasure ships. So it wasn't until late August 1590 that White finally managed to work his way across the Atlantic. He dropped anchor at the northeast end of Croatoan, a barrier island about 50 miles away from Roanoke, and . . .

"Croatoan!" I shouted. "Isn't that the . . . "

"Yes!" said the tour guide, clamping his beefy hand over my mouth. "And if you give away the ending, I'll make you sit in the back of the bus."

"Okay. Okay." I mumbled. "Tell the story your own way."

On August 15, 1590, White's ships reached the barrier island Hatoraske (now called Hatteras Island). The men could see smoke rising on Roanoke, which was not too far away. Oh, goodie, they thought. The colonists, who had been on their own for three years, were still alive. But it took White and his men three more days to reach Roanoke. First, Captain Spicer and six other men drowned when their boat capsized. They tried again, but then it was so dark that they overshot their mark by a quarter of a mile. Finally, on the morning of August 18, they stepped ashore on the north side of the island. What do you think they found?

"The colonists were having a cookout," I yelled.

The tour guide made a face. "No," he said. "Smoldering grass and burning trees."

"No colonists?"

"Not one."

So White and his men began to walk, but they found no sign of life except for three pairs of footprints left by Indians along the beach. White was starting to worry, but he still had hopes of finding the colonists *somewhere.* The men climbed a sandy bank that overlooked the settlement. Almost immediately they came upon a tree with the letters *CRO* carved into the trunk. They continued on to the site where the houses had stood. Not a single one remained, and the area was enclosed by what seemed to be a defensive barrier of tree trunks. White would later say it looked "very fortlike." But the only key to the mystery would itself become a mystery.

When White returned to Roanoke in 1590, he and his party found traces of the vanished colonists.

White saw that a patch of bark had been stripped from one of the trees in the defensive barrier. A single word had been carved into the smooth wood.

"Croatoan," I whispered.

"Yes," said the tour guide. "Croatoan, the very island at which White and his men had anchored that first night."

Did this mean that the settlers had moved the colony to Croatoan instead of 50 miles inland, as they had originally planned? The small boats that had been kept in the bay were missing, and the settlement site was heavily overgrown with weeds, suggesting it had been abandoned long before. Had the Indians attacked the settlement and forced the colonists

White discovers the inscription "Croatoan" on a tree on Roanoke Island. But what had happened to the missing colonists?

out? Was that why the colonists had built what appeared to be a defensive wall? It was possible, but White couldn't find any other signs that the colonists had been in distress.

Well, there was only one thing left to do. If they were going to unravel the mystery, White and his men had to go back to Croatoan Island. "We sail tomorrow!" he told them.

But it was not to be. A storm came up fast overnight, preventing the ships from attempting the short but dangerous crossing to Croatoan. So White opted to sail to the West Indies, pick up fresh water, and then come back. But that didn't work either. The unpredictable weather blew the ships far off course, landing them in the Azores, islands in the middle of the Atlantic Ocean.

That did it. Frustrated and exhausted, White and his men had had enough. They headed home to England, never able to return again to look for the little lost colony.

To this day, no one knows what became of the 125 settlers of Roanoke Colony. The barrier island of Croatoan no longer exists. The ocean has all but erased it, delivering its sands into the arms of Hatteras Island and Ocracoke Island. There is a lighthouse on Ocracoke and one on Hatteras. They send their beacons far into the night to the ships that long, long ago did not come in time.

The tour guide fell silent, and we all turned to look out over the water. And for a moment we, too, were as lost to the world as the colonists on Roanoke Island.

Books// Kent, Zachary. *The Mysterious Disappearance of Roanoke Colony in American History.* Berkeley Heights, NJ : Enslow Publishers, 2004.
This in-depth examination of the short history of the first British colony in America includes first-person accounts by people such as Sir Walter Raleigh.

Nardo, Don. *Atlantis.* San Diego, CA: Lucent Books, 2004.
From Plato's original account to modern theories, this book takes a thorough look at the legendary lost continent.

——. *Pyramids of Egypt.* New York: Franklin Watts, 2002.
Find out more about the pyramids of ancient Egypt.

Videos// *In Search of History: Lost City of Atlantis.* 50 minutes. New York: A&E Home Video, 2000. Distributed by New Video Group. Videocassette.
Find out what scholars and archaeologists think about the legend of Atlantis.

In Search of History: Lost Colony of Roanoke. 50 minutes. New York: A&E Home Video, 2000. Distributed by New Video Group. Videocassette.
This video explores various theories of the fate of the Roanoke colonists.

National Geographic Video: Into the Great Pyramid. 90 minutes. Burbank, CA: Warner Home Video, 2003. Videocassette.
This video covers recent archaeological work in Egypt. See the oldest known Egyptian coffin being opened and watch as a specially designed robot explores a shaft in the Great Pyramid.

Websites// *Atlantis—Fact, Fiction or Exaggeration?*
<http://www.activemind.com/Mysterious/Topics/Atlantis/>
Did Atlantis exist? Follow the links in this Web page to learn about the legend and the theories, then decide for yourself.

Roanoke: A Mystery in History
<http://www.thinkquest.org/library/site_sum.html?lib_id=2459&team_id=3826 >
This site has information on the world at the time of the Roanoke colony, the history of the colony, people involved with the colony, theories about the colony's disappearance, and more.

47

>> A6out the Author

Born in Baltimore, Maryland, Judith Herbst grew up in Queens, New York, where she learned to jump double Dutch with amazing skill. She has since lost that ability. A former English teacher, she ran away from school in her tenure year to become a writer. Her first book for kids was *Sky Above and Worlds Beyond,* whose title, she admits, was much too long. She loves to write and would rather be published, she says, than be rich, which has turned out to be the case. Herbst spends summers in Maine on a lake with her cats and laptop.

>> Photo Acknowledgments

Photographs and illustrations in this book are used with the permission of: © Llewellyn Publications/Fortean Picture Library, p. 7; © Scala/Art Resource, NY, pp. 9, 23; © CORBIS, p. 10; © Michael Nicholson/CORBIS, p. 12; © Bettmann/CORBIS, p. 14; © Karen Huntt Mason/CORBIS, p. 15; © William Donato/Fortean Picture Library, p. 16; © Kenneth Garrett, p. 18; © The Art Archive/Egyptian Museum Cairo/Dagli Orti, p. 19; © Klaus Aarsleff/Fortean Picture Library, pp. 20, 31; The British Museum, p. 22; © Claudia Adams/Root Resources, p. 24; © Mary Evans Picture Library, p. 25; © Yann Arthus-Bertrand/CORBIS, p. 27; © Roger Ressmeyer/CORBIS, p. 28; © North Wind Picture Archives, pp. 29, 34; Robert Schoch, p. 32; New York Public Library, pp. 35, 43; Courtesy of The North Carolina State Archives, pp. 37, 39, 44. Maps and illustrations by Bill Hauser, pp. 4–5, 8, 21, 36, 40.

Cover image by John Kreul/Independent Picture Service.